STAY IN THE GAME

No Adversity Is Too Great for You

JOEL OSTEEN

Faith
Words

NASHVILLE • NEW YORK

Also by Joel Osteen

STAY
IN
THE
GAME

FaithWords
Hachette Book Group
1290 Avenue of the Americas, New York, NY 10104
faithwords.com
twitter.com/faithwords

First Edition: July 2022

FaithWords is a division of Hachette Book Group, Inc. The FaithWords name and logo are trademarks of Hachette Book Group, Inc.

The publisher is not responsible for websites (or their content) that are not owned by the publisher.

The Hachette Speakers Bureau provides a wide range of authors for speaking events. To find out more, go to www.hachettespeakersbureau.com or call (866) 376-6591.

Library of Congress Cataloging-in-Publication Data
Names: Osteen, Joel, author.
Title: Stay in the game : no adversity is too great for you / Joel Osteen.
Description: First edition. | Nashville : FaithWords, 2022.
Identifiers: LCCN 2022004295 | ISBN 9781546029335 (hardcover) |
    ISBN 9781546029311 (ebook)
Subjects: LCSH: Christian life. | Perseverance (Theology) | Resilience
    (Personality trait)—Religious aspects—Christianity.
Classification: LCC BV4509.5 .O868 2022 | DDC 248.4—dc23/eng/20220302
LC record available at https://lccn.loc.gov/2022004295

ISBN: 9781546029335 (paper over board), 9781546029311 (ebook)

Printed in the United States of America

LSC-C

Printing 1, 2022

Contents

Introduction

My friend Dale Brown, the legendary coach of the LSU basketball team, told me about the time he was speaking to a group of soldiers at a military base in California. When he finished, a young man came up to him who stood nearly seven feet tall and weighed 250 pounds.

"Coach Brown," the young man said, "I want to try out for our basketball team, but I can't dunk the basketball. I can barely jump. When I run up and down the court, my legs tire out so quickly that I can only play a few minutes."

"How long have you been in the military, son?" Coach Brown asked him, gazing up at him, then down at his size-seventeen shoes.

"I'm not in the military, Coach. My father is. I'm thirteen years old."

Coach Brown immediately decided to take this young man under his wing. He said, "When I get back to Louisiana, I'm going to send you my training program. It will help strengthen your legs and increase your endurance."

Three months later, he got a letter from the young man saying, "Coach Brown, I've done everything you've asked me to do, spent hours in the gym and in the weight room working out. But my basketball coach just cut me from the team. He told me that I'm too big, too slow, too clumsy, that I'll never be able to play basketball." Nothing but negative labels were stuck to him.

Coach Brown wrote him back and said in effect, "Son, if you just stay in the game, keep working out, keep being your best each day, and keep asking God to help you, He will get you to where you're supposed to be."

That young man had to make a decision. "Am I going to wear these negative labels throughout

my life? 'Too big.' 'Too slow.' 'Too clumsy.' Or
am I going to follow the dream that God has
placed in my heart? Am I going to think better
and live better? Am I going to believe I'm a giant
killer and I can do all things through Christ?"
He decided to remove the negative labels and stay
in the game.

That young man, Shaquille O'Neal, ended up
going to LSU and playing college basketball for
Coach Brown, where he broke all the records and
became one of the greatest basketball players who
ever played the game. Today there is a bronze
statue of Shaquille—the clumsy kid who could
barely jump—dunking the basketball in front
of the LSU Tigers basketball practice facility. I
wonder where he would be now if he had believed
the negative labels, if he had thought, *My coach
is right. I guess I am too big, too slow, too clumsy.*
We wouldn't be talking about his nineteen-year
NBA Hall of Fame career today.

Perhaps you feel like Shaquille did. You've
been told what you can't do, what you don't

have, how you'll never be good enough. It's easy to get discouraged, throw in the towel, and give up. But nothing that was spoken over you has to define you, and nothing that's happened in your past has to keep you from your destiny. God has designed you specifically for the race that you're in. He is saying to shake off the discouragement, stay in the game, and move forward with your life.

As you read these pages, I'll help you put on a new attitude and get back in the game. Keep fighting the good fight of faith, and one day soon you won't just be in the game, but you'll be living the life of victory that you didn't think was possible.

1

Stay in the Game

It's easy to have a good attitude and pursue your dreams as long as everything is going your way. That doesn't take a lot of faith. But what about the difficult times when a relationship doesn't work out, you get a bad health report, or a friend does you wrong? It's easy to lose your passion when you are hurting. Many people are sitting on the sidelines of life because they're injured. They are nursing their wounds and not moving forward because of what they've been through.

You may have a reason to feel sorry for yourself, but you don't have a right. God promised to give you beauty for those ashes. He said He would pay you back double for the wrongs, but you have to do your part. If you are to see the beauty, if you're to get double, you have to shake off the self-pity. Shake off the discouragement and get back in the game. We all have wounds, but you can't let a loss, a health issue, or a divorce be your excuse to sit on the sidelines. Sometimes in life you have to play in pain.

This thought struck me while I was watching a football game in which one of the best players had a broken hand and bruised ribs. He was a big offensive lineman. He wasn't expected to play. The trainers wanted him to sit the game out, but he wasn't about to miss it. He had a big cast on his arm and he was wearing a special vest to protect his ribs. He was so bandaged up he looked like a mummy.

A reporter asked him how he felt: "It's a little painful, but I'd rather be in the game in pain than sitting on the sidelines watching."

If you are to become all God created you to

be, you can't let an injury, hurt, or disappointment cause you to sit on the sidelines, either. Be
like that banged-up lineman. Bandage what's
hurting. Forgive the person who did you wrong.
Let go of what didn't work out and get back in
the game.

Have a Made-Up Mind

I met a lady I hadn't seen in a long time in our
church lobby. She's an older woman, very faithful, attends our services regularly. I said in passing, "I haven't seen you lately. Where have you
been?"

She said, "Joel, I had emergency surgery. I've
been in the hospital for three months."

"Wow! We're so glad to have you back," I said.
"How are you doing?"

For as long as I live I will never forget her
words.

She said, "I'm hurting, but I'm here."

That's the kind of people God rewards. Faithful people. People who are determined. People who get knocked down, but don't stay down. Instead, they get back up again. You can't let the hurt, the pain, or the bad break cause you to be bitter, or to lose your passion, or to start blaming God. As this lady from our church did, you need to stay in the game.

No matter what life deals your way, your attitude should be: *I'm hurting, but I'm still here. A friend did me wrong, but I'm still here. Business is slow, but I'm still here. I didn't feel like coming, but I'm still here.*

You need to make up your mind to stay in the game. You can't just be faithful only as long as you feel perfectly well, as long as everybody treats you right, or as long as it's sunny and cool outside. You have to be like this lady with a made-up mind. "I'm hurting, but I'm still coming."

"My boss did me wrong, but I'm still getting to work on time, being my best."

"My child won't speak to me. It's breaking

my heart. I'm in pain, but I'm still singing in the choir. I'm still ushering each week. I'm still being good to a friend in need. I've still got a smile. I'm still giving God praise."

Anybody can sit on the sidelines. Anybody can find an excuse to be sour, to drop out, or to give up on life. I'm asking you to stay in the game. When you're hurting and in pain, it's easy to become fixated on the hurt, the disappointments, the bad breaks. All that will do is bring more discouragement, more self-pity, eventually even depression.

One of the best things you can do when you're hurting is go out and help somebody else who is hurting. Get your mind off your problems and pain by helping somebody else in need. When you help others in your time of need, you are sowing a seed God can use to change your situation.

This was what my mother did in 1981, when she was diagnosed with terminal liver cancer. She was given a few weeks to live. She didn't feel well. She had a good reason to be discouraged. She could have gone home, pulled the curtains, and been depressed. She could have sat on the sidelines. Nobody would have faulted her. But my mother understood this principle. She stayed in the game. She would drive across town to pray for a sick friend. The truth is she needed prayer more than that friend, but my mother was sowing a seed. She would come to church every weekend and pray for other people in need. She was hurting, but she was still in the game.

Scars into Stars

God has a greater reward for people who are faithful in the tough times. When my sister Lisa was in her early twenties, she went through an unwanted divorce. She was so devastated. It was an unfair situation. For weeks she was so depressed that she wouldn't leave the house.

Most of the time, she wouldn't even come out of her room. In the morning, she couldn't wait for it to get dark. At nighttime, she couldn't wait for the morning. She wasn't living, just existing.

One day Lisa called my father and she was crying. She said, "Daddy, I think I'm having a nervous breakdown." She was in so much pain. She was overwhelmed.

Our family tried to cheer her up. We tried to encourage her, but we couldn't get her out of that deep hole of depression. A minister friend, T. L. Osborn, called Lisa and said, "Nobody can bring you out of this except you. You know I love you, Lisa, but you have to quit feeling sorry for yourself. Quit nursing your wounds. Quit thinking about your problem. Get out of the house and move forward with your life."

Lisa was defensive at first, almost offended. She was thinking, *You don't know the pain that I'm feeling. You don't know what I'm going through. This has ruined my life.*

"Lisa, if you'll move forward," he said, "God

will take your scars and turn them into stars for His glory."

When Lisa heard that, something came alive inside. It's as though a stronghold was broken in her mind. Instead of sitting at home feeling sorry for herself, she went to the church and started a class every week for people who were believing for their marriages to be restored. She reached out to other people who were hurting. She was injured, but she got back in the game. Through her actions she was saying, "I'm hurting, but I'm still here. I'm disappointed, but I'm still here. They did me wrong, but I'm still here."

Lisa could have remained bitter with a chip on her shoulder, blaming God, but she made the decision to get back in the game. Today, more than thirty years later, she's happily married, with a great husband and three beautiful children. She saw what God promised. He took the scars and turned them into stars. He gave her beauty for those ashes. But it all happened when she made the decision to get back in the game.

Arise

The prophet Isaiah put it this way: "Arise from the depression in which the circumstances have kept you. Rise to a new life." Notice, if you want a new life there's something you have to do. You can't sit back in self-pity. You can't wait until all your wounds heal and you feel 100 percent. You have to do as Lisa did and arise from that discouragement.

Shake off what didn't work out. Quit mourning over what you've lost. Quit dwelling on who hurt you and how unfair it was, and rise to a new life. When God sees you in the game, pain and all, bandages and all—when you show up with the attitude: *I'm hurting, but I'm still here. I'm hurting, but I know God is still on the throne. I'm hurting, but I'm expecting God to turn it around*—that's when the Creator of the universe goes to work. That's when God will pay you back for the wrongs that have happened to you.

You may be in a tough time. You may be sitting on the sidelines. If that's the case, God is saying, "Arise and get back in the game." If a friend betrayed you, don't go through life lonely. Go out and find some new friends. The right people are in your future. If you lost your job, don't sit around complaining. Go out and find another job. When one door closes, God will always open another door.

If you're facing a health issue, fighting a sickness, don't give up on life and start planning your funeral. Arise from that discouragement. When God sees you do your part, He will do His part. He will give you a new life. He will restore your health, give you new opportunities, new relationships. He will give you a new perspective. You will see that even though it's painful for a time, it is not the end. Even though it was unfair, it is not over. There is still life after the sickness, life after the divorce, and life after the bad break. A full life is still in front of you.

The Scripture says Job experienced this. He went through all kinds of tough times. He lost his children, his business, his influence, and his health. Everything that could go wrong did. He was tempted to sit on the sidelines of life. His wife told him, "Job, just give up. It's never going to get any better."

But in the midst of that pain, Job said, "I know my Redeemer lives." He was saying, in effect, "I'm hurting, but I'm still in the game. I'm hurting, but I know my God is still on the throne."

A year later when Job came through that challenge, God not only brought him out; God paid him back double for what he lost. The Scripture says, "After this, Job lived 140 years and saw his grandchildren down to four generations." Notice, after the trouble, after the loss, after the sickness, after the business went down, after the bottom fell out, his life still was not over. He didn't end on a sour, defeated note. He went on to live a blessed, happy 140 years, enjoying his grandchildren, accomplishing his dreams, fulfilling his destiny.

Your life is not over because you had a setback. God has an "after this" in your future. When you go through tough times, don't be surprised if the enemy whispers in your ear, "You'll never be as happy as you used to be. You've seen your best days. This setback is the end of you." Let that go in one ear and out the other. God is saying to you what He said to Job: "After the cancer, after the bad break, after the disappointment, there is still a full life." You have not danced your best dance. You have not laughed your best laugh. You have not dreamed your best dream.

If you stay in the game and do not grow bitter, God will bring you out just as he brought out Job. He will bring you out with double what you had before.

Play in Pain

There was a pro football player whose younger brother was tragically killed in an accident the day before a big game. This player had practically raised his siblings. They were extremely close. You can imagine the pain and shock he must have been in. The coach told him to go back home and spend as much time as he needed with his family. But he said, "No, Coach. I'm playing in the game tomorrow in memory of my brother. I know that's what he would want me to do."

It's interesting that this player had one of the greatest games of his career. He caught an incredible touchdown pass and made other great plays. Some people would see it as a coincidence, just the adrenaline of the moment. But I see it as the hand of God. I believe God was saying, "If you dare stay in the game, if you dare play with pain, I'll breathe My favor on your life."

Nobody would fault you for being discouraged when you are nursing your wounds over a lost loved one, a serious illness, a child with special needs, or a legal battle. That's what most people expect. But when you defy the odds, play in pain, and say, "Hey, I'm hurting, but I'm still here," the most powerful force in the universe breathes in your direction.

You may be in a difficult time. You could easily be discouraged. But God is saying, "It's time to wipe away the tears. Wash your face. Put on a new attitude and get back in the game."

You may not be able to do what you used to. You may have some aches and some limitations. That's all right. God is not necessarily concerned about your performance. He is looking at the fact that you're in the game.

You could have a chip on your shoulder. You could be sitting on the sidelines. It takes an act of faith to ignore the voices giving you excuses to sit there. When you refuse to listen to them and get back in the game, God sees your effort. God knows what it took for you to come to church or to reach out to someone else in need.

Other people may not know the battles you had to fight to get back in the game. They don't understand the discouragement you had to overcome. They didn't see all the opportunities you had to get sour and throw in the towel. Just the fact that you showed up says to God, "You are still on the throne." You're saying to yourself, "I'm in it for the long haul." And you're saying to the enemy, "You're under my feet. There's nothing you can do to keep me from my destiny."

When Jesus was here on this Earth, He felt every pain, every emotion, that we would ever feel. He knows what it's like to be lonely, to go through a loss, to be betrayed, and to be discouraged—so much so that His sweat became like great drops of blood in the garden of Gethsemane. He's been where we are. The Scripture says, "He is touched with the feelings of our infirmities."

When you hurt, God feels the pain. You're His most prized possession. You're His child. When you arise in spite of the pain and get in the game, that's the seed God will use to take the scar and turn it into a star.

Get God's Attention

I met a man in the Lakewood Church lobby who was wearing a wristband from the hospital. I asked him if everything was okay. He explained that he'd had surgery earlier that week, a major surgery. He was supposed to stay in the hospital through the weekend to recover. But he said, "Doctor, I have to go to church on Sunday. I'm an usher. They'll be expecting me."

The doctor said, "No way. I'm not even thinking about letting you out of the hospital. You're staying right here and recovering."

The man said, "Doctor, you don't understand. I have to be at church. I never miss a Sunday."

The doctor looked at him and said, "Let me ask you. Do you go to Lakewood?"

He said, "Yes, sir. I do."

The doctor said, "Lakewood people are the most dedicated, faithful, happiest people I've ever seen." Then he said, "I'm going to make a deal with you. I'm going to give you a three-hour pass to go to church on Sunday morning and then you get right back in here and get in that bed to recover."

The man showed up. He was hurting, but he was here. He told me before the service, "Joel, don't go long. I'll get in trouble!"

There's another younger man who attends Lakewood services. He always has a smile, seems as happy as can be. What I didn't realize was that he had been on dialysis for twelve years. I took my father to dialysis the last three months of his life. I know a little bit about that. It's not always easy. It can be a burden. This young man always wore long-sleeved shirts. One Sunday he came up for prayer. I met him at the altar for the first time. I said, "Hey, I see you out there in the audience all the time. It's good to finally meet you."

He said, "Yeah, Joel. I never miss a service. I love coming." He rolled up his sleeve. His whole arm was as red as a tomato. It looked like somebody had taken an ice pick and poked at it for three hours straight. I'd never seen anything like that before.

I couldn't help but think about all the times I had seen him out in the audience with his arms up in the air in worship. It looked like he didn't have a problem in the world. He looked as happy as could be. What I didn't realize was that under that sleeve he was injured. He was here, but he was hurting. He was playing in pain.

It's one thing to go through a difficulty that everybody knows about. You're worried, discouraged. You have your friends and family members praying. There's nothing wrong with that. We're all human. We all have emotions. We handle things in different ways.

But what really gets God's attention is when you're in a tough time, you're hurting, you're in pain, but like this young man, you're so stable, you're so consistent, you're so at peace, nobody knows anything about it. You show up to church each week with a smile. You go to work with a good attitude. You're kind, friendly, and compassionate. The whole time you're fighting a battle that nobody knows anything about. That gets God's attention in a great, great way.

About three months later the young man who'd been on dialysis so long came back to the altar with another young man. He said, "Joel, my friend is donating one of his kidneys to me. I'm receiving a transplant on Tuesday."

The procedure went great. The new kidney responded perfectly. Today, he's not on dialysis anymore. He doesn't have to wear long-sleeved shirts anymore. He's healthy, free from that pain. Twelve years after the start of dialysis, after the struggle, after the pain, there was still a bright future in front of him. Because he stayed in the game, as Job did, he came into his "after this." God will do the same thing for you.

Don't Sit on the Sidelines

There's a young lady in the Scripture who went through a time of great pain because her husband died. Her name was Ruth. In a moment, her life forever changed. Ruth could have easily given in to self-pity or discouragement, feeling that life was just not fair. But Ruth stayed in the game. She chose instead to look after her mother-in-law, Naomi, who was widowed and had lost both her sons.

Naomi said, "Ruth, you're a young woman. I'm an old lady. You have a full life in front of you. Don't worry about me. Go back to your mother's home, and may the Lord grant you to find rest in the home of another husband."

Ruth said, "No, Naomi. I'm not leaving you by yourself, especially when you're hurting. I'm going with you and taking care of you." Even though Ruth was hurting, even though she was in pain, she reached out to somebody else who was hurting.

Month after month, Ruth just kept taking care of Naomi, finding ways to get the food they needed, serving her dinner, being her friend. One day Ruth was out in the harvest fields doing the hard work of gathering up the grain the harvesters had missed. She met this man named Boaz. He was the owner of all the fields, the wealthiest man in that area. They fell in love and got married. God blessed them with a baby boy. They named him Obed.

Obed had a son named Jesse. Jesse had a son named David. David, of course, went on to be the king of Israel, one of the greatest men to ever live.

Ruth could have sat on the sidelines the rest of her life after that loss, but she understood this principle: She played in pain. She was injured, but she kept doing the right thing. God had an "after this" for Ruth. After the loss, after the pain, God said, "I'll give you a great-grandson who will change the world."

You may be in pain today. Maybe you've suffered a loss, been through a disappointment. My message is, "That is not the end. God still has a plan." Don't sit around nursing your wounds. Don't let bitterness and discouragement set the tone for your life. God is saying, "Arise. Wipe away the tears and get back in the game."

Have the attitude: *I'm hurting, but I'm still here. I'm disappointed, but I've still got a smile. They did me wrong, but I'm still giving God praise.*

If you stay in the game, God will always have an "after this" for you. After the loss, you'll meet the right person. After the layoff, you'll get a better job. After the sickness, you'll come out stronger. After the disappointment, you'll still live a blessed, full, happy life. Just like my mother. Just like the young man with the kidney. Just like Ruth, like Job.

I believe and declare, in spite of the pain, in spite of the adversity, because you're still in the game, God is going to make the rest of your life the best of your life.

2

Keep the Right Perspective

We all face challenges, but it's not the size of the problem that's important. It's our perception of that problem. It's how big or small we make it in our minds.

When Moses sent twelve men to spy out the Promised Land, ten came back and said, "We'll never defeat the inhabitants. There are giants in the land. They live in fortified cities." But the two other spies, Joshua and Caleb, came back with a different report. They said, "Yes, the people are big, but our God is bigger. We are well able to take the land. Let us go in at once."

Both groups saw the same giants and the same situation; the only difference was their perspective. One group focused on the size of their God; the other group focused on the size of their enemy. Out of the two million people camped next door to the Promised Land, only two made it in, Joshua and Caleb.

Could it be that your perspective is keeping you out of your promised land? If you see your challenges as impossible and you tell yourself, "I'll never get out of debt, and I'll never overcome this sickness, and I'll never accomplish my dreams," then just like them, your wrong perspective can keep you from becoming all God's created you to be.

What you focus on, you magnify. If you stay focused on your problem or what you don't have and how it will never work out, all you're doing is making it bigger than it really is. When you magnify something, you don't change the size of the object; you only change your perception of it. That was why David said, "Magnify the

Lord with me." He was saying if you want to make something bigger, then don't make your problems bigger, don't make the medical report bigger, don't make the opposition bigger. Learn instead to make God bigger.

When David faced Goliath, he never called him a giant. Everybody else did. They talked about his size, his strength, and his skill. But David called Goliath "an uncircumcised Philistine." He never even gave Goliath credit for being that big. Here's the key: David didn't deny it, but he didn't dwell on it. His attitude was: *If I'm magnifying anything, I'm magnifying the source of my strength. I'm talking about God's greatness. I'm not focusing on how big my problems are. I'm focusing on how big my God is.*

His brothers and the other Israelite soldiers were afraid and ran away from Goliath, wondering what they were going to do. When David told them he wanted to fight Goliath, they said, "You can't fight him—you're just a kid, you're too small, you don't have a chance." But David had a different perspective. He knew if God be for him, who would dare be against him? He knew he was strong in the Lord. David knew he wasn't alone, that all the forces of Heaven were backing him up. They tried to warn him: "David, you're going to get out there and get killed. Goliath is too big to hit."

David said, "No, he's too big to miss." He went out, stood before Goliath, and said, "You come against me with a sword and a shield, but I come against you in the name of the Lord God of Israel!" David was magnifying his God, talking about God's goodness. This teenage boy—half the giant's size with no chance in the natural—defeated this huge giant. How? He had the right perspective.

Don't Be Intimidated

Philippians 1:28 says, "Do not be intimidated by your enemies." You may be like David, up against a big giant right now—a giant of debt, a giant of sickness, a giant relationship struggle, a giant legal problem. It's so big that it looks impossible in the natural. You could easily be overwhelmed and think, *I don't have a chance.* No, God is saying, "Don't be intimidated. Those for you are greater than those against you." Put your shoulders back and hold your head high. You are not weak, defeated, or powerless. You are a child of the Most High God, anointed, equipped, well able. Don't you dare shrink back and think, *It's just too big. It's been this way too long. My career is never going to take off. I'll never break this addiction. I'll never accomplish my dreams.*

Do as David did—get a new perspective. You are full of can-do power. The greatest force in the universe is breathing in your direction. There is no challenge too tough for you, no enemy too big, no sickness too great, and no dream too far off.

The same power that raised Christ from the dead lives inside you. The enemy would not be fighting you so hard if he didn't know God had something great in store. I've found the size of your challenge is an indication of the size of your future. If you are facing a big giant challenge, don't be discouraged. That means God has something amazing just up in front of you. He has a new level of your destiny.

Do you know what made David king? Goliath. God used the opposition to take him to the throne. When you face great difficulties, it's because God wants to take you to your throne. He wants to take you to a higher level. Your challenge may have been meant for your harm, but God wants to use it to your advantage. That giant is not there to defeat you; it is there to promote you. You may be in tough times, but the right perspective to have is: *I'm not staying here. I'm coming out. This too shall pass. I'm not buried; I'm planted. I may be down, but I'm coming up stronger, better, increased, promoted, and at a new level.*

That is what it says in Exodus about the people of Israel when they were enslaved to the Egyptians:

"The more opposition, the more they increased."
When you face adversity, don't get depressed and
say, "God, why is this happening to me? I thought
Joel said this would be a good year. I went to church
last Sunday." Your attitude should be: *I know this
opposition is a sign that increase is headed my way. It
looks like a setback, but I know it's really a setup. It
will not be a stumbling block to take me down. God
will use it as a stepping-stone to take me up.*

Have an Attitude of Victory

As with David, you need to have an attitude of
victory. Sometimes we're talking to God about
how big our problems are, when we should be
talking to our problems about how big our God is.

I love the way David responded to Goliath
when the giant was laughing and making fun of
him for being so small. Goliath said, "Am I a dog
that you would come at me with a stick? Don't
you have anything better than this little runt?"

David looked him in the eyes and said, "This day I will defeat you and feed your head to the birds of the air." He didn't say, "I hope so," "I believe so," or "I'm praying about it."

Your declaration should be: "I will have a blessed year. I will beat this addiction. I will come out of debt. I will live healthy and strong. I will fulfill my God-given destiny." You may be up against big opposition, but don't be intimidated by that medical report, don't be intimidated by that legal situation, and don't be intimidated by the size of your dream.

One of our Lakewood Church visitors told me she was in Houston for treatments, but she had such a positive attitude I found it hard to believe she was facing a serious illness. She told me "Everything is fine," and she wouldn't even say the word *cancer*. She would not give the disease credit for what it was. She wasn't denying it. She was choosing not to dwell on it. Her attitude was: *I'm not intimidated. This cancer is not bigger than my God. He made my body. He controls my destiny. No weapon formed against me will prosper. If it's not my time to go, I'm not going.* She had the right perspective. She didn't let the disease define her or dominate her life.

Her story reminded me of this little boy I heard about. There was a big bully from down the street who was always bothering him. The boy was trying to get his nerve up to stand up to the bully, but he was too afraid.

One day his father bought him a new telescope. He was out in the front yard playing with it, but he was looking through the wrong end. He was looking through the big side.

His father came out and said, "Son, you're doing it backward. Turn it around and it will make everything bigger like it was meant to do."

The little boy said, "I know that, Dad. But right now I'm looking at this bully. And when I look at him this way, it makes him so small that I'm not afraid of him anymore."

You may need to turn the telescope around. You've magnified that problem long enough, you've thought about how impossible it is, and how it's never going to work out. But if you turn it around, you'll see it from the right perspective; you'll realize it's not a problem for God. All He has to do is breathe in your direction.

It's Under Your Feet

First Corinthians 15 says, "God has put all things under our feet." You need to see every obstacle, every sickness, every temptation, and every bad habit as being under your feet. It's no match for you. It's not permanent. It won't keep you from your destiny. It's already defeated, and it's just a matter of time before you walk it out.

You won't struggle with that addiction for your whole life. It's under your feet. That depression that's been in your family for so many years won't be passed to the next generation. It's under your feet. You're putting a stop to it. That struggle, lack, barely getting by, is not permanent. It won't keep you from being blessed. It's under your feet. It's just a matter of time before you break through to a new level.

You need to shake off the lies that are telling you: "It's too big, I've had it too long, and it's never changing." This is a new day. God is saying, "No enemy, no injustice, and no obstacle will defeat you. They will promote you instead." Your challenge wasn't meant to be a stumbling block to take you down, but God is using it as a stepping-stone to take you higher. Keep the right perspective. It's under your feet.

David said in Psalm 59, "I will look down in triumph on all of my enemies." Notice he doesn't say "some of my enemies," but "all of my enemies." What am I going to do? "Look down in triumph." Why am I looking down? "Because they're under my feet."

You may be facing obstacles that don't feel like they're under your feet. That sickness seems big, that financial problem looks impossible, or maybe you've had the addiction for years. But you can't go by what you see. You should go by what you know. We walk by faith and not by sight. In the natural it may feel huge, but when you talk to that enemy as an act of faith, you need to do as David did and look down. It's under your feet. When you talk to that sickness, that depression, that fear, look down. I've heard that if you want to say something to the enemy, write it on the bottom of your shoe, because he's under your feet.

Can-Do Power

Sometimes when there's a big boxing match, the two fighters will face each other the day before the fight at a press conference. They'll stand toe to toe, with their faces just two or three inches apart. They'll look each other in the eye, staring, each trying to intimidate the other. They're saying, "I'm tougher, stronger, bigger, meaner. You're not going to defeat me."

When you face an enemy, something that's

trying to keep you from your destiny—a sickness, a bad habit, an unfair situation—unlike these two fighters, you don't stand toe to toe to look that enemy in the eye. That enemy is not at your level. It may have a big bark. It may seem larger and tougher, like you'll never defeat it. But the truth is, it's no match for you.

For you to look it in the eye, you need to look down under your feet. You are more than a conqueror. If God be for you, who dare be against you? The enemy has limited power, but our God has all power. He said greater is He that's in you than he that comes against you.

Now quit telling yourself, "I'll never get out of debt. I'll never lose this weight. I'll always struggle in this area." Change your perspective. You are not weak, defeated, or inferior. You are full of can-do power. The same spirit that raised Christ from the dead lives in you. You have to start putting some things under your feet.

God said, "I've given you power to tread on all the power of the enemy." Notice that word *tread*.

It has to do with a shoe. One translation says it means "to trample." If you start seeing those enemies as under your feet, as trampled, as already defeated, you'll rise up with a new boldness and your faith will activate God's power in a new way.

The prophet Isaiah said, "No weapon formed against you will prosper." He doesn't say that you won't have difficulties. That's not realistic. Challenges will come, people will talk about you negatively, you may get a negative medical report, or a family member may get off course. God said the problem may form, but you can stay in peace knowing that it won't prosper against you. That means it won't keep you from your destiny. Because you belong to Him, and because you dwell in the secret place of the Most High God, He has put a hedge of protection around you, a hedge of mercy, a hedge of favor that the enemy cannot cross.

No person, no sickness, no trouble, no bad break, and no disability can stop God's plan for your life. All the forces of darkness cannot keep you from your destiny. When you're in difficulties and you're tempted to be upset, you need to remind yourself, "This problem may have formed, but I have a promise from Almighty God that it's not going to prosper. They may be talking about me, trying to make me look bad. But I know God is my vindicator. He'll take care of them. My child may be running with the wrong crowd, but it's not permanent, it's temporary. As for me and my house, we will serve the Lord. The medical report may not look good, but I know God made my body. He has me in the palms of His hands and nothing can snatch me away."

Armed with Strength

I read an article about scientists who were researching Alzheimer's disease. They studied the brains of those who had died with the disease and compared them to the brains of those who had died without it. They found that many people had lesions on their brains that technically qualified as Alzheimer's disease, but the interesting thing was that when they were alive, they showed no signs of Alzheimer's. Scientifically they had it, but the symptoms never showed up. Their minds were sharp. Their memories were excellent.

The common denominator was that these people were positive and hopeful, and they stayed productive. The prophet Isaiah said just because the problem forms doesn't mean it has to prosper. We may have things that come against us because of our genetics, things that were passed down, but the good news is that God can override it. God has the final say.

That's what happened with Ramiro. He was born with no ears. The doctors told his parents he would never be able to hear or speak. The problem had formed. In the natural it didn't look good, but we serve a supernatural God.

Ramiro had parents who believed his disability didn't have to prosper. They didn't sit around in self-pity thinking, *Poor old us*. They knew they were armed with strength for the battle. They knew God put it under their feet. They just kept praying, believing, and speaking faith.

When Ramiro was a few months old, the doctors noticed that even though he didn't have ears, parts of his eardrums had formed. These incredibly gifted doctors performed a surgery to create ears for him and correct the problem. He got a little better, had more surgeries, and improved even more. Today, Ramiro can not only hear and speak, he can also sing. He's a worship leader at Lakewood, and he appeared on *American Idol* singing "Amazing Grace" in front of millions of people.

Whatever you're facing, it's under your feet. It's not permanent, it's temporary. The power that is for you is greater than any power that will be against you. Keep the right perspective. Turn that telescope around. Don't focus on the size of the problem; focus on the size of your God. He's brought you through in the past, and He will bring you through in the future. The problem may have formed, but it will not prosper.

I speak strength into you. I speak healing, determination, new vision, favor, wisdom, and courage. I declare you will not be intimidated. You are strong, confident, and well able. This is a new day. The tide of the battle is beginning to turn. You will not be overcome; you are the over-comer. You will not be the victim; you are the victor. God will not only bring you out, He will bring you out better off than you were before.

3

You Can Handle It

We all go through disappointments, challenges, and unfair situations. It's easy to let it overwhelm us to where we think, *This is too much. I can't deal with this illness. I can't handle this difficult child. I can't take this traffic. This relationship issue is going to be the end of me. It's driving me crazy. I give up. It's over.*

God would not have allowed it if you couldn't handle it. But as long as you're telling yourself it's too much, you'll talk yourself out of it. Have a new perspective. You are not weak. You are full of can-do power. You are strong in the Lord. All through the day, whether you're stuck in traffic or facing a major disappointment, your attitude should be: *I can handle it. I can handle this grouchy boss. I can handle this difficult child. I can handle these people talking about me behind my back. I can handle this legal situation.* You can't have a weak, defeated mentality. You have to have a warrior mentality.

This is what Joseph did. He was betrayed by his brothers, thrown into a pit, sold into slavery and taken to a foreign country, and spent years in a prison for something that he didn't do. But he didn't get depressed. He didn't start complaining. His attitude was: *I can handle it. God is still on the throne. He wouldn't have allowed it unless He had a purpose for it, so I'm going to stay in faith and keep being my best.* In the end, he was made second in charge over all of Egypt. No person, no bad break, no disappointment, and no sickness can keep you from your destiny.

My mother was diagnosed with terminal liver

cancer in 1981 and given just a few weeks to live. She could have fallen apart and said, "God, it's not fair. I've served You all these years, and I have all these children to love and care for. I don't understand it." Instead her attitude was: *I can handle it. I'm not a victim. I'm a victor. Nothing can snatch me out of God's hands.* Today, forty years later, my mother is still going strong, healthy, full of joy, full of peace, and helping others.

My father, back in the 1950s, was the pastor of a large denominational church. His future looked very bright. They had just built a beautiful new sanctuary. But through a series of events, my dad had to leave that church. It was a major setback, a big disappointment. He had given years of his life there. But he didn't sit around nursing his wounds. His attitude was: *I can handle it. I know when one door closes, God always opens up another door.* He and my mother went out and launched Lakewood Church, and here we are today still going strong.

"Take Hold of His Strength"

The apostle Paul put it this way: "I have strength for all things through Christ who empowers me" (Philippians 4:13). Listen to his declaration: "I am ready for anything. I am equal to anything through Him who infuses strength into me." Paul was stating, "The enemy may hit me with his best shot, but it won't stop me. I'm more than a conqueror."

Paul knew what he was talking about. He had been shipwrecked, spent the night on an open sea, and gone days without food. He was falsely accused of crimes, beaten with rods, and thrown into prison. He had people coming into the churches he founded who were lying about him and preaching another gospel. If anyone had a right, at least in the natural, to be negative, bitter, and complain, it would have been Paul. But he understood this principle. His attitude was: *I can handle it. I am ready for and equal to it. Why?*

Because Almighty God, the Creator of the universe, has infused me with strength. He has equipped me, empowered me, anointed me, crowned me with favor, put royal blood in my veins, and called me to reign in life as a king.

In difficult times you have to talk to yourself the right way as Paul did. If you don't talk to yourself, your thoughts will talk to you. They will tell you, "It's too much. It's never going to change. It's not fair. If God loved you, He would have never let this happen."

The Scripture says, "The rain falls on the just and the unjust." Just because we're a person of faith doesn't exempt us from difficulties. Jesus told a parable about this where one person built their house on a rock. They honored God. Another person built their house on the sand. They didn't honor God. What's interesting is that the same storm came to both people. The wind blew and the rain fell on both houses. The difference is that when you honor God, the storm may come, but when it's all said and done, you will still be standing. The other house built on the sand was washed away. The enemy may hit you with his best shot, but because your house is built on the rock, his best will never be enough. When the storm is over, you will not only come through it, but you'll come out stronger, increased, promoted, and better than you were before.

Now you have to do what Paul did. Shake off a victim mentality and have a victor mentality. You're not a weakling. You're not lacking. The most powerful force in the universe is breathing in your direction. Every morning you need to remind yourself, "I am ready for and equal to anything that comes my way. I am full of can-do power. I am strong."

That sickness is no match for you. That relationship issue is not going to keep you from your destiny. The loss of that loved one did not stop God's plan for your life. Don't let it overwhelm you. You can handle it. You've been armed with strength. When you have this warrior mentality, this attitude of faith, knowing that you've been equipped and empowered, all the forces of darkness cannot stop you.

The prophet Isaiah said, "Take hold of His strength." When you make this declaration, "I can handle it," that's not just being positive. You're taking hold of strength. When you say it, you're getting stronger. That's why the Scripture says, "Let the weak *say*, 'I am strong.'" Listen to what you're saying to yourself. "I can't stand this job." "This professor is so difficult. I'll never pass his course." "My loved one didn't make it. I don't know what I'm going to do." If you're always talking about the problem, all that's doing is draining you. When you talk defeat, strength is leaving. Energy is leaving. Creativity is leaving. Quit letting those things overwhelm you. You are not a victim. You are a victor. If it came your way, you can handle it. You are ready for it and equal to it. If you stay in agreement with God, He will take what is meant for your harm, and He will use it to your advantage. That difficulty won't defeat you. It will promote you.

Walk Through the Fiery Test

I read about a businessman who had worked for a large home improvement company for over thirty years. They had retail stores all over the country. He helped build that business from the ground up. But one day they had a corporate restructuring. They decided that they no longer needed him. Of course, he was disappointed. It didn't seem fair. But instead of sitting around nursing his wounds, thinking about what he'd lost, he had the attitude: *I can handle it. This is not going to defeat me. It's going to promote me.*

In difficult times you have to remind yourself that nothing is a surprise to God. He's not up in the heavens scratching His head, saying, "Oh, man, he got laid off. That messed everything up." "Oh, she was diagnosed with cancer." "Joseph got thrown into a pit. Now what am I going to do?" God knows the end from the beginning. He has already written every day of your life in His book. The good news is, if you stay in faith, your book ends in victory.

This executive, instead of looking for another job, got a couple of his friends together, and they started their own company. They called it "The Home Depot." It's become one of the largest, most successful home improvement stores in the world. What am I saying? That difficulty is not meant to defeat you. It's meant to promote you. A setback is simply a setup for a greater comeback.

"Well, Joel. It's so hard, and I don't understand it. It doesn't seem fair."

You're talking yourself into defeat. If it came your way, you can handle it. Start talking to yourself in a new way. "I am well able. I am equipped. I am empowered. I am ready for anything."

The fact is that God is not going to deliver us from every difficulty. He is not going to keep us from every challenge. If He did, we would never grow. The Scripture says, "Our faith is tried in the fire of affliction." When you're in a tough time, that's an opportunity to show God what you're made of. Anybody can get negative, bitter, and blame God. It's easy to lose your passion. But if you want to pass the test, if you want God to take you to a new level, you can't be a weakling. You have to be a warrior. Dig your heels in and declare with Paul, "I can handle it. I'm ready for it. I'm equal to it. I know God is still on the throne. He is fighting my battles, and on the other side of this difficulty is a new level of my destiny."

Colossians 3:12 says, "God has given us the power to endure whatever comes our way with a good attitude." Maybe at the office you're not being treated fairly. It's one thing to go to work negative, discouraged, complaining, and bad mouthing the boss. That doesn't take any faith. But if you want to pass the test, you have to go to work with a smile on your face, with a positive attitude, being good to people, doing more than you're required. At your home, maybe your spouse is not treating you the way they should. It's easy to think, *I'm going to treat him the way he is treating me.* Or, *These kids are disrespectful. I'm not going to give them the time of day.* But if you want to pass the test, you have to be good to people even when they're not being good to you. You have to do the right thing when the wrong thing is happening. See it as an opportunity to grow. Every time you do the right thing, a blessing will follow. When you take the high road, there will always be a reward.

Too often the mistake we make is to constantly tell ourselves, "It's not fair. It's not right. When they change, when it improves, then I'll have a better attitude." You have to make the first move. You do your part, and God will do His part. Quit worrying about God changing another person, and first allow God to change you. Is there something you're letting overwhelm you? You have to stop thinking it's too much. Get up every morning and make this simple declaration: "God, I want to thank You that I can handle anything that comes my way today. I can handle a difficult boss. I can handle getting stuck in traffic. I can handle my plans not working out. Lord, thank You that I'll have a good attitude wherever I am." You have to decide before you leave the house that nothing that comes your way is going to upset you. Decide ahead of time.

All Things Will Work Out for Your Good

A friend of mine was going to have her family over for dinner on Christmas Eve, and then they were going to her in-laws' for a Christmas Day lunch. She was in charge of bringing desserts for both parties. She is a very organized, detailed person. A couple of weeks before Christmas, she called her favorite bakery, where she had ordered desserts many times before. This time she ordered seven pies: one lemon meringue, two pecan, two pumpkin, and two chess pies. She had to work on the morning of Christmas Eve, and in the afternoon she was going to drive with her mother to the bakery and pick up the pies. But that day a snowstorm unexpectedly came in. The roads were very difficult to travel. The whole city was frozen over. Nevertheless, she and her mom braved the bad weather. They finally made it to the bakery just before it closed on Christmas Eve.

My friend walked up to the counter, handed the young man her receipt, and said, "I'm here to pick up my seven pies."

He shook his head and said, "I'm sorry, ma'am. We don't have any more pies."

She said, "That's impossible. I ordered these two weeks ago. I have to have these pies for my Christmas dinners."

He repeated, "I'm sorry. The weather was so bad that we didn't think anybody else would come in, so we sold all the pies."

She was very upset. She started telling her mother how wrong that was and how she was going to call the owner, how it was ruining her Christmas, on and on.

Another customer had come in behind them and overheard everything that was going on. This lady walked up to my friend with a big smile and said, "Hey, it's Christmas. Why are you so upset? I'm going to pray that you find your desserts."

My friend rolled her eyes and thought, *Lady, I don't need prayer. I need pies.* She thanked the lady for praying, then she and her mother exited the bakery and got back in the car.

Her mother said, "Why don't we call the other bakery across town?"

Exasperated, my friend replied, "Oh, Mom, we'll never get across town in this bad weather. Besides, they're not going to have any pies left late on Christmas Eve." Her mother finally talked her into calling the bakery. When she asked if they had any pies, the lady said, "Let me check." She came back on the line and said, "All we have left are seven pies: one lemon meringue, two pecan, two pumpkin, and two chess."

God is in complete control. You don't have to get upset when things don't go your way. You have the power to remain calm. You can handle any situation. Quit letting little things steal your joy. Every day is a gift from God. Life is too short to live it negative, offended, bitter, and discouraged. Start passing the tests. Start believing that God is directing your steps. Believe that He is in control of your life. Believe that He has solutions to problems that you haven't even had. If you stay calm and stay in faith, God promised that all things will work out for your good.

"Well, Joel," you say, "I was in that same type of situation, but it didn't have a good end. They didn't have any pies left." Maybe God is trying to help you lose some weight. You can handle it!

Things Will Not Stick to You

We've all seen how a spider spins a web in order to catch an insect. That web is filled with a sticky substance, so when an insect comes in contact with it, it not only gets tangled in the web, but it actually gets stuck. Have you ever wondered how the spider that's spinning the sticky web can walk across it and not get stuck? It seems as though it would get trapped in its own web. But God made the spider so that its body releases a special oil that flows down to the legs. That way it can just slide across the web. You could say the spider doesn't get stuck because of the anointing that's on its life. In a similar way, God has put an anointing on your life. It's like oil that causes things not to stick.

When you walk in your anointing, knowing that you can handle anything that comes your way, things that should bring you down won't be able to. You get laid off. It wasn't fair. You should be discouraged. You should be upset, but you stay in faith and you end up with a better job. A relationship comes to an end. You should be bitter, should be discouraged, but you keep moving forward, and God opens up a new door. At the office, people are playing politics, talking behind your back. You should try to get even. You might try to pay them back, but because of this anointing, it just slides right off you.

Perhaps you wonder, as I did, *How did I make it through the loss of my father?* How did you make it through that slow season at work? How did you make it through that illness, that breakup? It's because of the anointing God put on your life. He gave you strength when you didn't think you could go on. He gave you joy when you should have been discouraged. He made a way when it looked impossible. Now we can all say with David, "Where would we be without the goodness of God?" Bottom line: God has infused strength into you. He has equipped and empowered you. You are ready for and equal to anything that comes your way. When you face difficulties, remind yourself, "I am anointed for this. I'm not going to fall apart. I'm not going to start complaining. I can handle it. I know that God is still on the throne. He is fighting my battles, and if God be for me, who dare be against me?"

I have a friend who has had cancer three times. I've never once heard him complain. I've never seen him depressed. We used to play basketball together. Nobody even knew anything was wrong. He doesn't have a weak, defeated, "poor old me" mentality. He has a warrior mentality. He knows he can handle it. He's anointed for it. A couple of years ago, the cancer came back for the third time. The doctors told him that before he took chemo they were going to harvest his white blood cells, which they could use to help restore his immune system after the treatment. He asked the doctors how many of these cells they needed. They gave him a number. He said, "Doctors, I'm going to give you twice what you need."

For the next couple of months, all through the day he would go around saying, "Father, thank You that my white blood cells are multiplying. They're getting stronger, increasing. They will do exactly what You have created them to do." What was he doing? Talking to himself. Taking hold of that strength.

He went back to the doctors, who said, "You're a man of your word. You've given us four times the amount that we were hoping for." He took that treatment, and today he is totally cancer free, healthy, and strong.

Refuse to Give Up

Remember that the Scripture says in Philippians, "Do not be intimidated by your enemies." Don't be intimidated by that cancer. It's no match for you. Sickness cannot keep you from your destiny. God has you in the palms of His hands. Nothing can snatch you away. If it's not your time to go, you're not going to go. Don't be intimidated by that financial problem. Don't be intimidated by what somebody said about you. There is an anointing on your life that seals you, protects you, enables you, and empowers you. God has infused you with strength. The Scripture calls it can-do power.

I was at the beach one time when our children were little. Alexandra was three years old, and Jonathan was six. We were having a good time, playing in the sand, making castles, when this little yellow bumblebee came and landed right beside Alexandra. She took off running, afraid. I swatted the bee out of the way. We went back to playing. About thirty seconds later, that bumblebee was right back flying all around. My kids started screaming, "Daddy! Get him! Get him!" I grabbed my towel and knocked him down to the sand. I thought, *I showed him who's the boss!*

About a minute later, there the bumblebee was again, buzzing all around, flying by our heads. This time I grabbed my towel and not only knocked him down to the sand, but I got my tennis shoe and squashed him into the sand as hard as I possibly could. I was tired of dealing with him. We went back to playing. A couple of minutes later, I looked over just to make sure he was still dead. I couldn't believe it. I noticed one wing start to move. Then the other wing came up out of the sand. I thought, *This is the bumblebee from Hell*. He started walking across the sand as though he was dazed. I was amazed that not only was he alive, but that he could get back up again. About that time, he started flying off away from me.

Just when I thought he had learned his lesson—"Don't mess with Joel"—that bumblebee turned around and came right back and buzzed by my head at least three or four times. I had to dodge to get out of the way. It was just like he was saying, "Ha-ha-ha! You couldn't kill me."

Alexandra exclaimed, "Daddy, kill him for good this time!"

I replied, "No, Alexandra. This bumblebee deserves to live. I'm a thousand times bigger than him, and I still couldn't keep him down."

That's the way you need to see yourself. No matter how big that enemy looks. No matter how powerful it may seem. There is a force in you that is more powerful than any opposition. Greater is He that is in you than anything that comes against you. Just be like that bumblebee—refuse to give up, refuse to fall into self-pity, refuse to let it overwhelm you. Instead, have this attitude: *I'm ready for and equal to anything that comes my way.*

I've been anointed with can-do power. I am armed with strength for this battle. When you have this warrior mentality, this "I can handle it" attitude, all the forces of darkness cannot keep you from your destiny.

Perhaps you've already decided, *I can't handle this sickness anymore. I can't handle this problem at work. I can't handle taking care of my elderly parents and my family, too.* Quit telling yourself it's too much. Those negative, defeated thoughts are draining your energy. You wouldn't be there if you couldn't handle it. God would not have allowed it if you weren't ready for it and equal to it. You're anointed for it. When you press past what's coming against you, on the other side of that difficulty is a new level of your destiny.

You Will Come Out Better

I heard about a wealthy man who was known for being very eccentric, far out. One night he was having a big party at his house. In his backyard, his swimming pool was filled with sharks and alligators. He announced to all the guests, "Anyone who will swim across my pool, I will give you anything that you want."

In a few minutes there was a big splash. He looked over, and this man was swimming ninety to nothing, dodging the alligators, maneuvering his way around the sharks, as frantic as can be. He made it to the other side just in the nick of time and jumped out totally panicked.

The wealthy man came over and said, "I can't believe it. You're the bravest person I've ever met. Now, what do you want me to give you?"

The man looked around the pool and answered, "What I want more than anything else is the name of the person who just pushed me in!"

Here's my point. Sometimes in life it feels as though we got pushed in. We weren't expecting it. A bad medical report. The relationship didn't make it. A business goes down. It may be a surprise to us, but it is not a surprise to God. If you get pushed in, don't sit around nursing your wounds. Do as this man did and just go for it. Just keep being your best. Keep honoring God. Keep doing what you know you're supposed to do. God has already given you the strength, the wisdom, the favor, and the determination not only to make it through, but to come out better than you were before.

Remember, that difficulty is not going to defeat you. It's going to promote you. You can handle it. Take hold of this strength. Get up every morning and remind yourself, "I'm ready for and equal to anything that comes my way. I am strong." If you do this, God promises He will infuse strength into you. You will overcome every obstacle, defeat every enemy, and live the victorious life that belongs to you.

4

Your Second Wind Is on the Way

We all grow tired sometimes, tired of trying to make a business grow, tired of dealing with a sickness, tired of raising a difficult child, tired of being lonely and waiting to meet the right person. We can even be doing what we love, whether it's living in the house of our dreams, raising great children, or working at a good job, but if we're not careful we can lose our passion and allow weariness to set in.

I watched a documentary about a long war involving our country. The United States troops had been overseas for many years engaged in conflict. A four-star general testified before Congress. A senator asked how the troops were doing. He said, "Sir, our troops are tired. We never expected the war to go on this long. Now they're dealing with battle fatigue."

The military was facing the same question we often face as individuals: What do you do when the battle has lasted longer than you thought it would? You've prayed. You've believed. You've done what you're supposed to, but you're still waiting to meet the right person. Or you're still looking for the right job. Or you're still praying that a child you care about will get back on track.

The word *weary* means "to lose the sense of pleasure, to not feel the enjoyment that you once felt." When soldiers are first sent overseas, they're excited. They can't wait to make a difference. Then when the battle goes on and on, fatigue can set in. The same can happen to any of us who've been fighting for something over a long period.

The problem is that when you allow yourself to become weary, you'll be tempted to quit—to quit growing, to quit standing for that wayward child, to quit believing that you'll become healthy and whole, or to quit pursuing your goals and dreams.

A woman visiting our church told me that she was in town for a checkup at the big cancer center in Houston, and she hadn't received the news she'd hoped for. She'd gone through six months of chemotherapy. She was hoping she was done, of course. She found out that the chemo had done some good, but they told her she needed another six months of treatments. She was so disappointed. She said, "Joel, I'm tired. I don't think I can do this for six more months."

On the way to our victories we will always face the weariness test. We will be tempted to become discouraged and give up. The test never comes when we're fresh. It never comes when we first start out. It always comes when we're tired. That's when we're the most vulnerable.

Faint Not

The apostle Paul said in Galatians 6:9, "Don't grow weary in doing what's right, for in due season you shall reap if you faint not." Two words are the key to this whole passage: *faint not.* In other words, if you don't give up, if you shake off the weariness, if you put on a new attitude knowing that God is still in control, if you dig your heels in and say, "I've come too far to stop now," if you "faint not," you will see the promise come to pass.

Instead of complaining about how long the battle is taking, we should say, "This too shall pass. I know it's not permanent. It's only temporary. I'm not camping here. I'm moving forward."

Weariness kept the people of Israel out of the Promised Land. They were close to their victory, next door to the Promised Land. God had already said He would give them the land. All they had to do was go in and fight for it. But they allowed weariness to set in. They had gone through the wilderness, overcoming obstacles, defeating all kinds of enemies. Then they grew tired. Moses tried to get them to go in, but weariness leads to discouragement.

When you're discouraged, you see the problem instead of the possibility. You talk about the way it is instead of the way it can become. The people of Israel started complaining: "Moses, our enemy is too big. We don't have a chance. We'll never defeat them."

They made a permanent decision based on a temporary feeling. If you allow yourself to become weary and you lose your passion, you, too, will be tempted to make decisions based on how you feel rather than based on what you know.

When you feel that weariness come on, you need to pray to build strength. "God, You said You have armed me with strength for every battle. You said I can do all things through Christ who infuses inner strength into me. You said I am more than a conqueror, a victor and not a victim." If you talk to yourself the right way, you will feel the second wind kick in.

But too often we do as the people of Israel did and think, *I can't take this anymore. I'm so tired. I'm so run-down. It's just too hard.* Yet, the more you talk about how tired you are, the more tired you become. You're just adding fuel to the fire. Don't talk about the way you are. Talk about the way you want to be.

You need to have words of faith and victory coming out of your mouth. In other words, "This may be hard, but I know I'm well able. I'm equipped. I'm empowered. I am strong in the Lord."

Find New Strength

We all grow tired. We all become weary. In fact, if you never feel like giving up, your dreams are too small. If you never feel like quitting, you need to set some larger goals. When that pressure comes to be discouraged and to think you can't take it anymore, that is completely normal. Every person feels that way at times.

The prophet Isaiah gives us the solution. He said, "Those who wait on the Lord will find new strength. They will soar high on wings like eagles'. They will run and not grow weary. They will walk and not faint."

God knew there would be times when we would feel battle fatigue. That's why He said, "There is a way to get your second wind. There is a way to have your strength renewed. What is it? Wait on the Lord."

One translation says, "Hope in the Lord." That doesn't mean to sit around and be passive, complacent. It means to wait with expectancy, not complaining, not discouraged, not talking about all the reasons why it won't work out.

If you want your strength renewed, the right way to wait is by saying, "Father, thank You that You are fighting my battles. Thank You that the answer is on the way. Thank You that You are bigger than these obstacles. Thank You that You are bringing my dreams to pass."

When you give God praise, you talk about His greatness; you go through the day expecting Him to turn it around. God promises He will renew your strength. The Scripture says, "You will run and not get weary." This is a reference to catching your second wind. That's God breathing strength, energy, passion, vision, and vitality back into your spirit. You won't just come out the way you were. You will come out on wings like eagles'. You will come out stronger, higher, better off than you were before.

One Day at a Time

You may be up against major obstacles. When you look out into your future, it can be very overwhelming. You can't see how you will make it. I know a woman who was in the same situation. She raised her children and got them off to college. She was looking forward to this new season in her life in which she would have some free time. But because of unusual circumstances, she has had to raise her grandson, who is just a toddler. Of course she loves her grandbaby, but she said, "Joel, I don't think I can do this again. Another fifteen years? I don't think I have the strength to make it."

I told her she can't focus fifteen years down the road. If she looks that far out, she will be overwhelmed. You have to take it one day at a time. You don't have the strength you need for tomorrow. When you get to tomorrow, you'll have the strength for that day.

But you can't think about struggling for years and years. Instead, focus on one day at a time. God asks only: "Will you do it today? Will you take hold of My strength today?"

Will you wait on the Lord today? Will you not give up and faint today? If you pass the test and do it today, then when you get to tomorrow the strength you need for that day will be there. As long as you worry—"How am I going to make it next week, or next month, or twenty years from now?"—that worry will drain your strength, drain your energy, drain your passion, and drain your victory.

All worry does is weigh us down and keep us from enjoying life. Instead of worrying about your future, get up every morning and say to yourself, "I can do this one more day. I may not know how I can do it the next twenty years, but I know I can do it for twenty-four more hours. I can stay in faith one more day. I can keep a good attitude one more day. I can have a smile on my face twenty-four more hours."

Take it one day at a time.

The End Has Been Set

I like to exercise to stay fit. Sometimes when I am out running, especially when it's hot and humid, I get tired. Those thoughts start coming, saying,

You need to stop. You're uncomfortable. It's hard, and look at how far you have to go.

The real battle takes place in our minds. If I dwell on those thoughts and start thinking about how I feel and how many hills there are and how far I have to go, I'll talk myself out of it and stop. Instead, I quit looking at the next two miles and just start telling myself, "I can do this one more step. One more step. One more step."

When I focus not on how far I have to go but instead on the next step, before long I look up and I'm almost there. I've pressed past the pain of being uncomfortable. I've found a rhythm, and all of a sudden my second wind kicks in, and instead of barely making it, I'm mounting up on those wings like eagles'. I'm finishing strong.

Thoughts will come to you: *It's never changing. You are never going to get well. You will never reach your goals.* But don't listen to them. God said in the book of Job that He has set an end to the difficulty. God has already established an end date for the trouble. He has set an end to the struggle, an end to the sickness, an end to the addiction, an end to the loneliness.

Remind yourself of that when you're in a difficult season and you feel the weariness creeping in, telling you, "It's not worth it. You're too uncomfortable. You have too far to go." Instead, remember, "I'm not always going to be lonely. God has set an end to this loneliness. He is bringing somebody great into my life."

"I won't always struggle in my finances. God has set an end to this lack. He has promotion and increase coming my way."

"I won't always be fighting these addictions. These bad habits won't trouble me my whole life. God has set an end to it. He has freedom and victory in my future."

"I won't always have to deal with these medical issues. There will not always be this pain. Jehovah Rapha, the Lord my healer, has set an end to this sickness."

Remember, the end has already been set. I'm asking you to stand strong. Don't grow weary.

Keep believing. Keep expecting. Keep being your best. If you stay on track and do what's right, you will see the end come to pass. That's what the Scripture means: "If you faint not, you will receive the reward."

It's No Match for You

I know you are not a fainter. You are strong! You are a warrior, a victor and not a victim. When life gets tough, remind yourself that God said you have been armed with strength for every battle. Think about that: God calls strength a weapon. In the natural you could be armed with a pistol, a hand grenade, or even a bazooka. Those are powerful weapons, but they are nothing compared to the weapons God has given you.

You are full of can-do power. Don't go around feeling weak and defeated and like you can't take it anymore. If it was too much for you, God wouldn't have allowed it.

Instead of complaining, tell yourself, "I can handle this. This child may be difficult, but I can handle it. Business may be slow, but I can handle it. The medical report wasn't good, but I can handle it. The boss is getting on my nerves, but I can handle it. It's hot outside, but I can handle it."

Put your shoulders back, look those obstacles in the eye, and say: "You're no match for me."

"Cancer, you're no match for me."

"Cranky coworker, you're no match for me."

"Depression, you're no match for me."

"Addictions, you're no match for me."

"Struggle and lack, you're no match for me."

"I know your end has already been set, and it's just a matter of time before God turns it around. It's just a matter of time before He brings that dream to pass."

A friend of mine is in the military, and he had just found out he would be deployed overseas for one year. He and his wife had never been apart for an extended time. They had two small children. His wife was very worried and wondered how she was going to make it.

I told her what I'm telling you: Your challenge may be difficult, but you can handle it. God has given you the grace for this season. If you weren't up to this, God wouldn't have brought it across your path. In tough times remind yourself there is always a reward for doing right. God never fails to compensate you. He pays very well. The season may be difficult right now, but if you keep doing the right thing, get ready. The reward is coming.

When you stand strong and have a good attitude, even though you really feel like complaining...

When you serve and give and treat people right, even when they're not saying "thank you"...

When nobody gives you credit...

When you pass these weariness tests, the Scripture says a payday is coming your way.

Keep Pressing Forward

You may be camped next to the Promised Land like the people of Israel, on the verge of stepping to a new level of God's favor, but the problem is you're tired. The battle has taken longer than you expected. You stand at a crossroads. You can either let that weariness weigh you down, causing you to give up and settle where you are, or you can dig your heels in and say, "I've come too far to stop now. I'll keep pressing forward. I'll keep pursuing my goals. I'll keep being good to people. I'll keep hoping, praying, stretching, growing."

When you have that kind of attitude, you will feel your second wind kick in. I've learned this: You face the greatest pressure when you are close to your victory. When the intensity has been turned up, that's a sign you're about to step to a new level of God's favor.

It's like a mother having a baby. When she faces the greatest pain, she is close to giving birth.

It's the same principle in life. When it's the most uncomfortable, when it seems the most unfair, when you're most tempted to give up, that's a sure sign you're about to give birth to the new thing God wants to do.

I can sense in my spirit the season is changing. The depression is coming to an end and joy is about to break forth. Your lack and struggle is coming to an end and a new season of increase, promotion, and more than enough is coming your way. If you've had constant medical problems and not felt up to par, that is coming to an end. A season of health, wholeness, and vitality is coming your way.

Now don't act like the people of Israel who became discouraged, too weary, and just wanted to settle where they were. Instead, press past the pain and discomfort. Press past the feelings telling you to settle. Press past the weariness. Get your fire back.

You have not seen your best days. Your greatest victories are still out in front of you. Those adversities and struggles will not go to waste. God is using them to prepare you for the amazing future He has in store.

Stand Strong

When I ran track in high school, our coach would give us unbelievable workouts. One time we had to run eighteen half-mile races. We would run a half a mile, take a two-minute break, and then run the next one. We had to do that eighteen times in a row. We thought, *This man is trying to kill us. There is something wrong with him.*

But several months later, we were all running at new levels and breaking our old records, and we realized he wasn't trying to kill us. He was simply increasing our endurance. He was stretching us so we could reach our full potential. In the same way God sometimes will allow us to face difficulties to increase our endurance, to stretch us so we can reach our full potential. We may think, *This is too hard. This boss is too unfair. This math teacher is too difficult. How can I raise these children?*

It may be very difficult. It may have been meant for your harm, but stand strong and declare, "I can handle this. It's not too much for me. I've been armed with strength for this battle." Then when you make it to the other side, you will not only receive your reward, you also will have an inner strength, a confidence, and a resolve you never had before.

You will face situations that might have been too much ten years ago. They might have caused you to be upset and fall apart. But because you've passed these tests, something has been deposited inside your spirit. What used to be a big deal is not a big deal at all.

What's happening? You're growing. You're increasing. You're stepping up to new levels.

I believe right now the Creator of the universe is breathing a second wind into you. Just receive it by faith. Strength is coming into your body. Strength is coming into your mind. You will run and not grow weary. You will walk and not faint. You will not drag through life defeated or depressed. You will soar through life on wings like eagles'!

5

Finishing Grace

It doesn't take a lot of effort to start things—a diet, school, a family. Starting is easy. Finishing is what can be difficult. Almost any young lady can have a baby, but it takes a mother to raise that child with love and care. Any two people can get married, but it takes commitment to stick with it for the long haul. Anyone can have a dream, but it takes determination, perseverance, and a made-up mind to see it come to pass.

The question is not, "Will you start?" but "Will you finish?" Will you finish the diet? Will you finish school? Will you finish raising your children? Many people start off well. They have big dreams. They're excited about their future. But along the way they have some setbacks. It's taking longer than they thought. Somebody didn't do what they said. Over time, they get discouraged and think, *What's the use? It's never going to work out.*

But God is called "the author and the finisher of our faith." He has not only given you the grace to start; He has given you the grace to finish. When you are tempted to get discouraged, give up on a dream, give up on a relationship, or give up on a project, you have to remind yourself, *I was not created to give up. I was not created to quit. I was created to finish.*

You have to shake off the discouragement. Shake off the self-pity. Shake off what somebody said. If you will keep moving forward in faith, honoring God, you will come into a strength that you didn't have before, a force pushing you forward. That's finishing grace. That's God breathing in your direction, helping you to become who He created you to be.

This grace is available, but you have to tap into it. It's not going to do us any good if we sit around in self-pity, thinking about how difficult it is, what didn't work out. "Well, my college professor is so hard. I'll never pass his course."

You have the grace to finish. Quit talking defeat and start talking victory. "I can do all things through Christ. I am full of wisdom, talent, and creativity. I will pass this course." When you do that, finishing grace will help you do what you could not do on your own.

Even in simple things. You start cleaning your house. Five minutes later, you think, *I don't feel like doing this. I am so tired. This is so boring.* Instead, turn it around and tell yourself, "I am strong in the Lord. I am full of energy. I am healthy. This is no match for me." If you tap into this finishing grace, you will vacuum your house as though you're on a mission from

God—vacuuming up dirt, coins, socks, children, anything else that gets in your way!

"He Will Bring You to a Flourishing Finish"

Maybe you're tempted to give up on a dream. Things haven't turned out the way you planned. It was going fine at first, but then you had some obstacles and you think, *It just wasn't meant to be.* Here's what I've learned. The enemy doesn't try to stop you from starting. He has seen a lot of people start. That doesn't bother him. But when you have a made-up mind and keep pushing forward, doing the right thing, taking new ground, when he sees you getting closer, he will work overtime to try to keep you from finishing. Don't get discouraged when you have setbacks, people come against you, or a negative medical report. That's a sign that you're moving toward your finish line.

The enemy was fine when you got started. He was fine when you were way back. No big deal.

But when you began to make progress, that got his attention. That's when he threw out some obstacles, some challenges. Where you confused him was when he thought you would give up after the first few difficulties. He thought you would get discouraged when that friend turned on you, when you lost that client, when your child got in trouble—but instead you kept moving forward, thanking God that He is in control, thanking Him that He is fighting your battles, thanking Him that no weapon formed against you will prosper. What were you doing? Tapping into finishing grace. When you should have gotten weaker, you got stronger. When you should have been depressed, you had a smile on your face. When you should have been complaining, you had a song of praise. Instead of talking about how big the problem was, you were always talking about how big your God is. When you should have gone under, God caused you to go over. When you didn't see a way, He made a way. When people came against you, He fought your battles and you came out better than you were before.

You may be up against challenges right now. It's because you are moving forward. You're making progress. Keep reminding yourself that God is the author and the finisher of your faith. He helped you to get started. That's great, but there's something more important: He is going to help you finish. He didn't bring you this far to leave you.

It says in Philippians, "God began a good work in you, and He will continue to perform it until it is complete." One translation says, "He will bring you to a flourishing finish"—not a defeated finish, where you barely make it and are beat up and broke. You are coming to a flourishing finish, a finish more rewarding than you ever imagined.

Be in It to Win It

In the Scripture, when Joseph was a teenager, God gave him a dream that one day he would rule a nation. His father, Jacob, loved him very much. Everything started off great for Joseph. He had a big dream, a supportive family. Life was good. But when Joseph was seventeen, things started to go wrong. His brothers became jealous of him and turned on him. They threw him into a pit and left him there to die. Eventually they changed their minds and sold him into slavery. He was taken to Egypt and resold to a man named Potiphar. Joseph hadn't done anything wrong, yet his whole world had been turned upside down. It looked as if his dream was dead, having been betrayed by his brothers and enslaved in a foreign country. If that wasn't bad enough, they put him in prison for years for something that he didn't do.

Joseph could have been depressed, angry, bitter, and upset. Nothing had turned out right. But Joseph understood this principle: He knew he had the grace not only to start but to finish what God had put in his heart. He knew the enemy wouldn't be fighting him if he wasn't heading toward his destiny. So he stayed in faith. He kept doing the right thing when the wrong thing was happening. He was not working unto people but working unto God.

One day Pharaoh, the leader of the nation, had a dream that he didn't understand. Joseph was able to interpret the dream. Pharaoh was so impressed with Joseph that he brought him out of prison and put him in charge of the whole nation. Joseph's dream came to pass.

God has put something on you that will override people being against you. It will override bad breaks and injustice. You have the grace not to just start. You have something even more powerful—the grace to finish. When you have an attitude like Joseph had, you cannot stay defeated. Life may push you down, but God will push you back up. People may do you wrong, but God will be your vindicator. Situations may look impossible, but God can do the impossible. When you have finishing grace, all the forces of darkness cannot stop you. You may have some setbacks, bad breaks, and injustice, but don't worry. It's only temporary. It's just a detour on the way to your destiny. That's a sign that you are moving toward your finish line.

The enemy doesn't fight people who are going the wrong way, people who are off course, discouraged, distracted, bitter, and angry. That's where he wants you. He comes against people who are headed toward the fullness of their destinies, people who are taking new ground, people like you who are coming into a flourishing finish. Our attitude should be: *I have a made-up mind. I am determined. I'm going to keep moving forward in spite of the bad break, in spite of the loss, in spite of the negative report, in spite of the critics. My destiny is too great and my assignment is too important to get discouraged, distracted, and bitter. I'm not going halfway or three-fourths of the way. I'm going to become all God has created me to be.*

When you're tempted to get discouraged and settle, it's because you're close to your breakthrough. You're close to seeing the problem turn around. You're close to meeting the right person. Pharaoh is about to call you, so to speak. The good break is on the way. The healing is on the way. The contract is on the way. Now you have to tap into this finishing grace. You've come too far to stop now. You've believed too long. You've worked too hard. You've invested too much. It may be difficult. Negative voices may be telling you, "It's never going to work out. Forget it. Just settle where you are." But don't believe those lies. You are close to your destiny.

When the going gets tough, you have to dig your heels in and say, "I am in it to win it. I am not moved by this opposition. I am not moved by what I see or by what I feel. I'm moved by what I know, and I know this: I have the grace to finish. I know this: God began a good work in me, and He is going to complete it. So I'm going to keep honoring God. I'm going to keep being good to people. I'm going to keep on being my best." Every day you do that, you are passing the test. You are one day closer to crossing your finish line.

Strength in Reserve

The Scripture says, "As your days are, so shall your strength be." This means your strength will always be equivalent to what you need. If you were to get a negative medical report, you're going to have the strength to deal with it. You're not going to fall apart. "Oh, I can't believe this is happening." Your strength will always match what you're up against.

When my father went to be with the Lord, my first thought was, *How am I going to deal with this?* My dad and I were very close. We had traveled the world together. All of a sudden he was gone. But what I thought would be very devastating and would knock the wind out of me wasn't anything like I had imagined. I felt a peace I had never felt, a strength, a resolve, a determination. I should have been upset and anxious, but that whole time I was at peace. Deep down I felt a rest. In my mind there were thoughts of worry, anxiety, and discouragement, but in my spirit I could hear God whispering, "Joel, I'm in control. It's all going to work out. I have you in the palms of My hands." That was finishing grace pushing me forward, propelling me into my destiny.

The psalmist said, "God is a very present help in times of need." In the difficulties of life, if you will get quiet and turn off the negative voices, you will feel a peace that passes understanding. You should be falling apart, but there is grace for every season.

Victoria and I were in Colorado one time, driving through the mountains. We rented a large SUV with an eight-cylinder engine. As long as we were on the flat roads, the engine was as quiet as can be. But as we started going up the steep winding mountain roads, just when you thought the vehicle couldn't make it, when it looked like it was going to stop, you could hear those extra two cylinders kick in. You could actually feel the car, almost as though it lifted up and took off with a new power.

Those two extra cylinders were there all the time. The extra power was always available. It just showed up when we needed it. It was strength in reserve. Sometimes in life we think, *How am I going to make it up that steep hill? I've gotten this far, but how am I going to deal with this illness? How am I going to raise this difficult child? I went through a loss, and I don't think I can go on.* The good news is that God has some strength in reserve for you. When you hit a tough time, don't worry. There are two more cylinders about to kick in, a strength you haven't tapped into yet. You're going to feel a force pushing you forward, taking you where you could not go on your own. That's finishing grace.

I've learned that the closer you get to your destiny, the tougher the battles become. The higher you go up the mountain, the more God promotes you, and the steeper the hill is. The critics will come out of the woodwork. People may not celebrate you. There will be unexpected challenges—a health issue, a business slows down, or you lose a loved one. It's easy to think, *I was doing so well. If I just wouldn't have had this bad break. Now I have this steep hill to climb.* That challenge is a sign that you are close to your destiny. The same God who gave you the grace to start is the same God who is going to help you finish. He knows exactly where your path is leading. Nothing you're facing is a surprise to Him. He knows every hill, every disappointment, and every setback. He said that His grace is sufficient. You will never come to a hill where you don't have the strength to climb it.

You may face some challenges, as I did when my dad went to be with the Lord, where you think, *I don't know how I'm going to make it up this mountain.* The reason you think that way is you haven't needed those two extra cylinders yet. You have not felt the full force of finishing grace. When it kicks in, it's going to propel you forward. You're going to climb mountains that you thought were way too steep. You're going to overcome obstacles that looked insurmountable, accomplish dreams that you thought were impossible. How could you do this? Finishing grace. You tapped into strength in reserve.

Guard Your Fire

This is what the apostle Paul did in the Scripture. He faced some huge hills. It didn't look as though he could fulfill his destiny. He was doing the right thing, sharing the good news, helping other people, but then he was arrested and put in prison. The closer he got to his destiny, the more obstacles he faced. He was alone, in a dungeon, on death row. It looked as though God had forgotten about him. But Paul wasn't defeated, depressed, or feeling sorry for himself. Even though he was in chains, they couldn't stop what God wanted him to do. Since Paul couldn't go out and speak publicly, he thought, *No problem. I'll start writing.* He wrote book after book. "Here's a letter to the Ephesians. Here's a letter to the Colossians, to the Romans, to the Corinthians." He wrote nearly half of the books of the New Testament, much of it from a prison cell. They thought they were stopping him, but they were doing just the opposite, causing his voice to become amplified. Here we are over two thousand years later, and we still feel Paul's influence. What they meant for harm, God used for good.

People may try to stop you, but finishing grace will get you to where you're supposed to be. They may push you down, but finishing grace will lift you back up. They may try to discredit, belittle, or leave you out. Don't get upset. They are a part of the plan to get you to your destiny. God will use them to propel you forward. As long as you stay in faith and keep honoring God, you will accomplish your assignment. He is the author and the finisher of your faith.

Now, quit focusing on who is against you, on how steep the hill is, on how impossible it looks. God has the final say. He brought Joseph out of prison. Paul stayed in prison, but they both fulfilled their destinies. If God doesn't turn it around the way you thought, He may cause you to have great influence right in the midst of your enemies as Paul did. In the midst of those difficulties, you can shine, be a bright light, and have God's favor. Bottom line is this: No person can stand against our God. No bad break can keep you from your destiny. God has given you finishing grace. He is going to get you to where you're supposed to be.

When Paul came to the end of his life, he said, "I have finished my course." One translation says, "I finished my course with joy." Notice, he didn't finish defeated, depressed, or sour. He finished with a smile on his face. He finished with a spring in his step. He finished with a song in his heart. That's what it means to have a flourishing finish.

We all have things come against us. It's easy to lose our passion and drag through life discouraged, negative, and bitter, but there is no victory if you finish your course that way. You have to make up your mind: *I'm not only going to finish my course; I'm going to finish it with joy, with a good attitude. Not complaining, but with a song of praise. Not thinking about what I don't have, but thanking God for what I do have. Not looking at what's wrong in my life, but thanking God for what's right in my life.* When you tap into finishing grace, you won't drag through the day. You will enjoy the day.

Thousands of years ago in Greece, there was a famous race called the Torch Race. All of the runners received a torch. At the start of the race, the runners would take off running with their torches lit. The only way you could win the race was to cross the finish line with your torch still lit. Even if you finished first, if your fire went out, you were disqualified. So the whole time they were running, on the forefront of their mind was protecting their fire, keeping it from wind or rain or anything that might put it out. They were constantly checking their torch to make sure that it was still lit.

It's the same principle in the race of life. If

you're going to finish your course with joy, you have to guard your fire. You can't let your flame go out. Too many people have lost their passion. They're still running, but their torch is no longer lit. At one time they were passionate about their dreams, then they had some setbacks. Now they're running, which is good, but they let their fire go out. They lost their zeal. If that's you, I've come to relight your fire. God is not done with you. You have not seen your best days. You have to shake off the blahs. Shake off the discouragement. There is a flame that is still alive inside you. The Scripture talks about how we must fan the flame, stir up the gifts. It's not enough to just finish. You have to finish your course with your fire still burning.

Finish Your Course with Joy

For as long as I can remember, my father struggled with high blood pressure. Toward the end of his life, he didn't feel well. The medicines made him dizzy. His kidneys quit working properly, and he had to go on dialysis. We used to travel overseas a couple of times a year. He really looked forward to it. But when his health went downhill, he had to stay at home and take dialysis three times a week. He never wanted to live if he couldn't preach. Even though he didn't feel well, he never missed a Sunday.

Victoria used to go pick him up and bring him to church a little bit late. Sometimes she would call and say, "Joel, I'm not sure your dad can minister today. It doesn't seem as though he feels well."

I would run down from the TV department during the service. When he arrived, I would ask, "Daddy, are you sure you're up to this?"

He would smile and say, "Yeah, Joel. I'm ready to go."

When he walked out on the platform, nobody knew he wasn't up to par. He still had a spring in his step, a smile on his face. He could have been at home, negative and complaining, "God, I've served You all these years. Look what it comes down to. I can hardly even minister."

Instead, he kept his fire burning. He guarded that flame. He was determined to not just finish his course, but to finish it with joy.

One night when my dad was seventy-seven years old, he wasn't feeling well. He asked my brother-in-law Gary to come over and visit with him. They were talking about two o'clock in the morning. Gary asked him what he thought about the difficulties he was having.

My father said, "Gary, I don't understand it all, but I know this: His mercy endures forever."

Those were the last words my father ever spoke. Right then, he breathed his final breath and went to be with the Lord. But think about those last words. He wasn't complaining. He was bragging on God's goodness. He was not magnifying his problem, but magnifying his God. He crossed the finish line with his fire still burning, with his torch still lit.

The Scripture talks about how the saints of old died in faith. The truth is that one day we're all going to die. You have to make a decision. Are you going to die in faith? Or are you going to die negative, bitter, and complaining, "I can't believe this happened"?

Make up your mind that you're going to die full of joy, with your fire still burning, with your torch still lit.

Never Give Up

In 1968, the Olympic Games were held in Mexico City. At less than the halfway point of the 26.2-mile marathon, a young runner named John Stephen Akhwari from Tanzania collided with another runner and fell to the ground, badly gashing his knee and causing it to dislocate. He also smashed his shoulder against the pavement.

He was bloodied and bruised, but after receiving medical attention, he somehow managed to get up and with sheer determination continued his race. More than an hour after the winner had finished the race, Akhwari entered the stadium for his final lap, despite the pain and severe leg cramps from the high altitude. More than one hundred thousand people had been there earlier, but now, an hour later, only a few thousand people remained in the stadium. The sun had set, and the television cameras were gone. The event was officially over.

As Akhwari struggled into the stadium and headed toward that final lap, when the few thousand people saw him limping and the bandage around his leg flapping in the breeze, they stood up and began to cheer him on. They cheered louder and louder as if he was in first place. Drawing strength from the crowd, he began to smile and wave as if he was going to win the gold medal. It was a moving moment, later seen around the world, and it became the great story of those Olympic Games.

A reporter asked him afterward, "Why didn't you drop out of the race when you were hurt? Nobody would have faulted you for it."

The young man's response has gone down in sporting history: "My country didn't send me five thousand miles to start the race. They sent me five thousand miles to finish the race."

In the same way, God didn't breathe His life into you, crown you with favor, and put seeds of greatness inside you just to start the race. He sent you to finish it. The Scripture talks about how the race is not for the swift or for the strong, but for those who endure till the end. You don't have to finish first. You're not competing with anybody else. Just finish your course. Keep your fire burning. You weren't created to give up, to quit. We can all find a reason to drop out of the race. We can all find an excuse. But you have to dig your heels in and say, "I am determined to finish my course."

If you tap into this finishing grace, those two extra cylinders will kick in when you need it. You'll have a strength that you didn't have. As did the apostle Paul, you will finish your course with joy. You will complete your assignment and become everything God created you to be.

About the Author

JOEL OSTEEN is a *New York Times* bestselling author and the senior pastor of America's largest church, Lakewood Church in Houston, Texas. Millions watch his weekly inspirational messages on television and connect with Joel through his digital platforms worldwide. Joel can be heard 24/7 on SiriusXM 128—Joel Osteen Radio. Connect with Joel on Facebook, Twitter, and Instagram or visit his website at joelosteen.com.

We Want to Hear from You!

Each week, I close our international television broadcast by giving the audience an opportunity to make Jesus the Lord of their lives. I'd like to extend that same opportunity to you. Are you at peace with God? A void exists in every person's heart that only God can fill. I'm not talking about joining a church or finding religion. I'm talking about finding life and peace and happiness. Would you pray with me today? Just say, "Lord Jesus, I repent of my sins. I ask You to come into my heart. I make You my Lord and Savior."

Friend, if you prayed that simple prayer, I believe you have been "born again." I encourage you to attend a good Bible-based church and keep God in first place in your life. For free information on how you can grow stronger in your spiritual life, please feel free to contact us.

Victoria and I love you, and we'll be praying for you. We're believing for God's best for you, that you will see your dreams come to pass. We'd love to hear from you!

To contact us, write to:

Joel and Victoria Osteen
PO Box #4271
Houston, TX 77210

Or you can reach us online at joelosteen.com.

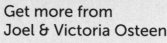

Stay connected, be blessed.

Get more from Joel & Victoria Osteen

It's time to step into the life of victory and favor that God has planned for you! Featuring new messages from Joel & Victoria Osteen, their free daily devotional and inspiring articles, hope is always at your fingertips with the free Joel Osteen app and online at JoelOsteen.com.

Get the app and visit us today at JoelOsteen.com.

JOEL OSTEEN
MINISTRIES

CONNECT WITH US